— MONSTER WARS —

ZOMBIES VS MUMMIES

CLASH OF THE LIVING DEAD

Michael O'Hearn

Consultant:
Michael Delahoyde, PhD

D1340127

Raintree

www.raintreepublishers.co.uk
Visit our website to find out
more information about
Raintree books.

To order:
☎ Phone 0845 6044371
🖹 Fax +44 (0) 1865 312263
✉ Email myorders@raintreepublishers.co.uk

Customers from outside the UK please telephone +44 1865 312262

Raintree is an imprint of Capstone Global Library Limited, a company
incorporated in England and Wales having its registered office at 7 Pilgrim
Street, London EC4V 6LB – Registered company number: 6695882

Editors: Aaron Sautter and John-Paul Wilkins
Designer: Tracy Davies
Media researcher: Eric Gohl
Production specialist: Eric Manske
Illustrator: Patricia Moffett
Originated by Capstone Global Library
Printed and bound in China by South China Printing Company

ISBN 978 1 406 24273 7 (paperback)
16 15 14 13 12
10 9 8 7 6 5 4 3 2 1

Acknowledgements
Alamy/AF Archive, 9 (bottom), 17 (bottom); Doug Steley A, 6 (right);
Photos 12, 10, 13; BigStockPhoto.com/John Salandiak, 6 (left); Szabo Balazs, 5
(bottom); Getty Images Inc./Pictorial Parade, 14; Kobal Collection/Hammer, 15;
Universal, 12; Mary Evans Picture Library/Ronald Grant Archive, 11; Amblin
Entertainment, 5 (top); Newscom/Album/Universal Pictures, 9 (top), 17 (top),
19 (left); Getty Images/AFP/Tim Sloan, 19 (right); Shutterstock/Danomyte
(mummy silhouette); Yuran (zombie silhouette).

British Library Cataloguing in Publication Data
A full catalogue record for this book is available from the British Library.

Disclaimer
All the Internet addresses (URLs) given in this book were valid at the time
of going to press. However, due to the dynamic nature of the Internet, some
addresses may have changed, or sites may have changed or ceased to exist
since publication. While the publisher regrets any inconvenience this may cause
readers, no responsibility for any such changes can be accepted by the publisher.

CONTENTS

WELCOME TO MONSTER WARS!

It's past midnight. The night is dark. Shadows creep across your bedroom wall. You swear they form a slit-eyed face. Floorboards creak. Trees outside your window groan. It's nothing, you tell yourself. But you lie awake ... watching ... listening ... waiting. You can't help but think a terrifying monster is hiding in your wardrobe.

In these pages, you'll learn the strengths and weaknesses of zombies and mummies. And you'll see them battle each other head to head. Will the zombies unravel the mummy when he climbs from his **tomb**? Or will the mummy unleash his revenge and send the walking dead back to the grave?

Are monsters real? No. But be ready for a creepy night-time battle.

tomb – grave or room that holds a dead body

THE FRIGHTENING TRUTH:

ZOMBIE VS MUMMY

Ancient Egyptians mummified their dead. They removed a dead body's organs, except for the heart. The body was then dried out with a type of salt called natron. Finally, the body was wrapped in linen cloth. The ancient Egyptians believed that preserving bodies in this way helped the dead live again in the afterlife.

In films and stories about mummies, curses and spells bring a mummy back to life. These mummies usually turn monstrous. They seek revenge on anyone who disturbs their tombs or gets in their way.

Zombies are also popular in stories and films. Zombies are walking corpses that have clawed their way out of their graves. A deadly virus often turns people into flesh-eating zombies. Each zombie spreads the virus, creating even more zombies. Sometimes poisonous sludge or radiation causes bodies to rise from the grave. Before long, the walking dead surround the living – and they're hungry for human flesh!

But which of these monsters is more dangerous? Read on to learn their undeadly secrets!

corpse — dead body
curse — evil spell meant to harm someone
radiation — rays of energy given off by certain elements
virus — tiny germ that infects living things

SPECIAL POWERS

Mummies can return to life when someone breaks into their tomb and reads an evil spell. The spell may also give the mummy powerful magic. Some mummies can control a person's mind or attack their enemies from far away. Sometimes, as they grow in power, they may look less like a mummy and more like a person. With a renewed body, they can move more easily among the living.

Zombies don't have magic. But their power is just as deadly. With just one bite, zombies can turn the living into the undead. If a zombie bites someone, that person becomes **infected** with the zombie sickness. If the person escapes without being eaten, the sickness will eventually kill him. After he dies, he'll rise again as a new flesh-eating zombie.

MUMMY magical abilities
★★★★

ZOMBIE deadly, infectious bite
★★★

infect — transmit a disease by introducing germs

INTELLIGENCE

MUMMY fairly clever
★ ★ ★

ZOMBIE dim-witted undead
★

Zombies often like to eat brains. But the brains in their own heads aren't very useful. Zombies can't think. They have only a dull **instinct** to eat fresh meat. They're always hungry, and they continually wander around looking for food. But they're not clever enough to look for places that have plenty of people to eat.

Mummies have no brains in their heads. But they're still clever. Mummies know what they want. They usually want to find a special magic book or treasure. And they won't think twice about killing someone to get it. In this battle of the brain-eater versus the brainless, the mummy has a definite advantage in brain power.

FRIGHTFUL FACT

Before wrapping a dead body, the ancient Egyptians used a hook to pull the brain out through the nose.

instinct — behaviour that is natural

STRENGTH

MUMMY magical power
★ ★ ★ ★

ZOMBIE average muscles
★ ★

Mummies are made to live forever in the afterlife. When they come back from the dead, they are magically strong. A mummy can lift a grown man by the neck and fling him across the room. Or he can crush a person's skull with his hands. A mummy has plenty of strength to defend himself from a pack of hungry zombies.

Shuffling undead zombies are only as strong as when they were alive. Their flesh also **decays**, which makes them weaker over time. When their bodies are damaged, they don't heal. But zombies do have one advantage. They can't feel pain. They just keep attacking until they are dead – again!

FRIGHTFUL FACT

Zombie films often centre on an end-of-the-world situation. In several films, scientists or the government accidentally create a sickness that causes an outbreak of the walking dead.

decay — break down or rot

SPEED

MUMMY stiff and sluggish
★

ZOMBIE slow, shuffling feet
★ ★

Zombies usually move slowly. They stagger and drag their feet. They may have broken bones, ripped flesh, and torn muscles. Zombies aren't likely to run down their victims. But when there are enough zombies, they can surround and trap victims, cutting off their escape.

Mummies move even more slowly than zombies. A mummy's body is usually thousands of years old. It's stiff and dried out, and wrapped tightly in cloth from head to toe. Rather than chase after people, mummies tend to surprise their victims and grab them from the shadows.

FRIGHTFUL FACT

Mummies have been found in countries around the world, including Chile, Denmark, Peru, China, and Japan.

WEAKNESSES

Mummies are usually brought to life by a curse that someone reads from a scroll. The scroll gives the mummy its power. Sometimes if the scroll is destroyed, the mummy dies. But the surest way to kill a mummy is with fire. Wrapped in so much dried-out cloth, mummies are like a match just waiting to be lit.

Destroy a zombie's brain and you kill the zombie. Whether it's a bullet or a blow to the head, zombies are fairly easy to kill. The problem is finding and killing all of them. As zombies spread their sickness, they multiply quickly. It's rare to find only a few zombies. Where there is one zombie, you're likely to find many of them.

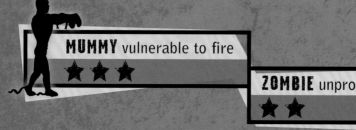

MUMMY vulnerable to fire
★ ★ ★

ZOMBIE unprotected brains
★ ★

FRIGHTFUL FACT

Mummies are often afraid of cats in films and stories. Cats were considered holy and were worshipped in ancient Egypt. Mummies are evil monsters, so cats are their natural enemy.

GET READY TO RUMBLE!

You'll hear their slow, staggering footsteps long before you see these undead foes clash. Can a zombie spread its sickness to a long-dead mummy? Will the mummy's strength and magic overcome a zombie attack? There are more questions than answers as this battle begins. But one thing is certain – one of these monsters will return to the grave. The other will keep bringing terror to all who cross its path.

Hide under the bed if you must, but don't stop reading. You have a graveyard seat for this monstrous battle. It's a clash of the living dead!

MUMMY

| ★★★★ SPECIAL POWERS | ★★★ INTELLIGENCE | ★★★★ STRENGTH | ★ SPEED | ★★★ WEAKNESSES |

ZOMBIE

| ★★★ | ★ | ★★ | ★★ | ★★ |

ONE LAST THING ...

The following fight is based on legends and stories. Walking undead zombies aren't real at all. Mummies are real, but they don't come back to life. However, you can still use your imagination. So dim the lights, turn the page, and get ready to be scared stiff!

CLASH OF THE UNDEAD

★ ★ ★ ★ ★ ★

The mummy slowly curls his fingers into a fist. He pounds his wrapped knuckles against the lid of the crate that holds him. The wood bends, then cracks, and finally bursts apart. The mummy sits up straight.

A dozen lightbulbs hang from the ceiling. They sway and light the room in a dim, shifting glow. The mummy stands stiffly. Strips of cloth hang from his body. He kicks away the broken pieces of his crate and stumbles towards a staircase.

His knees barely bend as he lumbers forward. Suddenly, a pale, limping zombie appears on the stairs.

The zombie trips and falls down the last few steps. His face is bruised and his nose is bent. He moans and sniffs the air. On his knees, he stares hungrily at the mummy.

The mummy stomps forward as the zombie climbs to its feet. The zombie stumbles towards the mummy, reaching out to grab his next victim. The monster grabs the mummy's arm and bites down with decaying teeth.

The mummy groans. He raises his arm and lifts the zombie off the ground. The zombie bites down harder. Suddenly, one rotted tooth snaps. Then a mouthful of blackened, yellow teeth break loose and rain to the floor. The zombie drops in a heap beside them.

The mummy reaches down and grabs the undead zombie. He flips the monster upside down and bashes it into a nearby crate up to its waist. Unable to attack, the stuck zombie kicks his legs slowly in the air.

The mummy climbs the stairs and reaches the deck of a ship. High above the deck, black smoke streams from a large chimney. Thick clouds cover the moon. The night sky is dim.

Skinny zombies dressed like sailors wander the deck aimlessly. The mummy stares at the strange creatures. One zombie chews on some rope tied to a lifeboat. Another bumps against a closed door trying to walk forwards. The ship presses on through the sea.

The zombies moan and stare blankly. They stagger towards the mummy. They claw at him and snap their jaws. One zombie grabs the mummy's cloth wrapping and tugs loose a strip of fabric. The mummy swats the tall, pale monster. He knocks the flesh-eater down, but the zombie holds tightly to the cloth.

The mummy bends stiffly and grabs his enemy by the neck. He lifts the creature high and throws it over the side of the ship. The zombie splashes into the water and sinks.

Now the mummy stands at the edge of the deck. A long piece of cloth drags behind him. Starving zombies crowd around him, grabbing and biting. The mummy raises his hand. Suddenly, a wall of sand magically appears and blasts across the deck. A dozen of the walking dead are swept off the ship and into the sea.

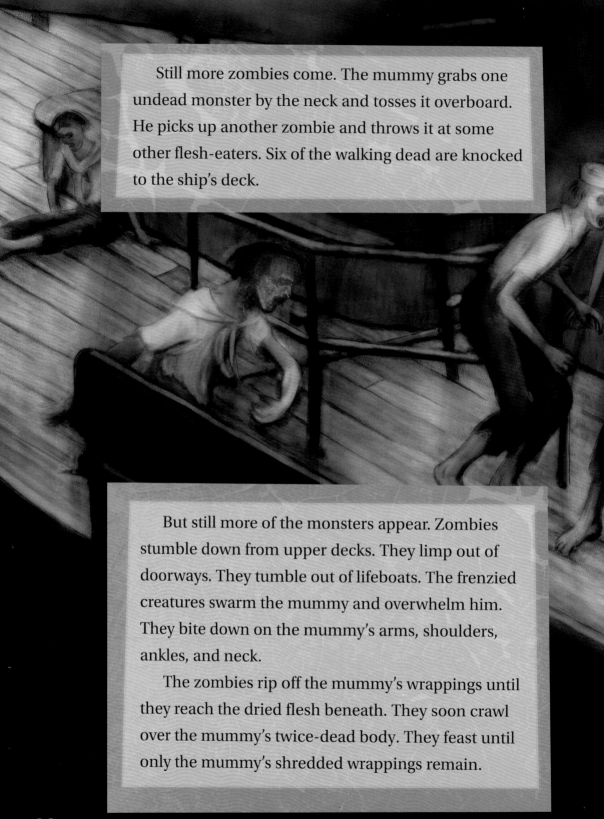

Still more zombies come. The mummy grabs one undead monster by the neck and tosses it overboard. He picks up another zombie and throws it at some other flesh-eaters. Six of the walking dead are knocked to the ship's deck.

But still more of the monsters appear. Zombies stumble down from upper decks. They limp out of doorways. They tumble out of lifeboats. The frenzied creatures swarm the mummy and overwhelm him. They bite down on the mummy's arms, shoulders, ankles, and neck.

The zombies rip off the mummy's wrappings until they reach the dried flesh beneath. They soon crawl over the mummy's twice-dead body. They feast until only the mummy's shredded wrappings remain.

GLOSSARY

corpse dead body

curse evil spell meant to harm someone

decay break down or rot

infect transmit a disease by introducing germs

instinct behaviour that is natural rather than learned

radiation rays of energy given off by certain elements

tomb grave, room, or building that holds a dead body

virus tiny germ that infects living things and can cause disease

FIND OUT MORE

BOOKS

The Ancient Egyptians: Dress, Eat, Write, and Play Just Like the Egyptians (Hands-on History), Fiona MacDonald (Crabtree Publishing, 2008)

Vampires, Werewolves, Zombies: Compendium Monstrum, Suzanne Schwalb and Margaret Rubiano (Peter Pauper Press, 2010)

Zombies on the Loose (Clash), Anne Rooney (TickTock Books, 2008)

WEBSITES

zombies.monstrous.com
Find out all you need to know about zombies on this website, including how to survive a zombie apocalypse!

www.bbc.co.uk/history/ancient/egyptians/ launch_gms_mummy_maker.shtml
Visit this BBC website to make your very own mummy.

INDEX